STRAY HOME

Stray Home

poems by Amy M. Clark

2009 Winner, Vassar Miller Prize in Poetry

University of North Texas Press
Denton, Texas

Permissions:
University of North Texas Press
1155 Union Circle #311336
Denton, TX 76203-5017

The paper used in this book meets the minimum requirements
of the American National Standard for Permanence of Paper for
Printed Library Materials, z39.48.1984. Binding materials have
been chosen for durability.

Library of Congress Cataloging-in-Publication Data

Clark, Amy M., 1966-
Stray home : poems / by Amy M. Clark. -- 1st ed.
p. cm. -- (Vassar Miller prize in poetry series ; no. 17)
"2009 Winner, Vassar Miller Prize in Poetry."
ISBN 978-1-57441-280-2 (pbk. : alk. paper)
1. Single women--United States--Poetry. I. Title. II. Series:
Vassar Miller prize in poetry series ; no. 17.
PS3603.L35543S77 2010
811'.6--dc22
2009045642

Stray Home is Number 17 in the
Vassar Miller Prize in Poetry Series

Contents

ACKNOWLEDGMENTS

I am grateful to the editors of the publications in which the following poems first appeared:

32 Poems: "Scope," "Why We Love Our Dogs"

The Cincinnati Review: "How to Be the Lady of the House"

Cream City Review: "Arc," "Calla Lily"

The Louisville Review: "Do You Want to Hold the Baby?"

Natural Bridge: "Dumb," "Stray Home, v-viii," (as "Bird Outside the Window")

Poet Lore: "Neighbors"

The Seattle Review: "Monkey with a Cup"

The Sow's Ear Poetry Review: "The Roasted-Corn Man of Golden Hill"

Tar River Poetry: "Night Rescue"

Tuesday; An Art Project: "Our Friends in Minnesota"

I wish to thank those who encouraged the writing of these poems, including Tom Berriman, Judy Bruton, Shirley Carroll, Angela Dale-Alexander, Amy S. Debrecht, Renee Fadiman, Jennifer Flescher, Dave Flietner, Lisa Fox, Bob Huttle, Draza Jansky, Erin Keane, Phuong Le, Bob Lowes, Richard Newman, Nancy O'Sullivan, Mike Perrow, Christine Portell, Nancy Powers, Eric Schramm, Susan Tchudi, Leslie Williams, and Roy Wooldridge.

Thank you, Molly Peacock and Jeanie Thompson, for your exquisite mentorship.

For your belief in this book, thank you, John Poch and Beth Ann Fennelly.

Thank you, Bill and Edie Clark, Jim Clark, Mary Baloian, and Emily Pakulski—always my biggest fans, and I yours.

And especially thank you, my beloveds, Jonathan Weinert and Jonah.

1.

Scope

A body on B Street
sleeps, pig-in-a-blanket,
while morning commuters
chuff at the stoplight,
then surge.

You have opened one eye
against the glass
of a scope and have seen
an egret balanced
on sling-back legs,
and have seen a city of bacteria
thrive in the smear on a slide.

The sleeper's blanket
shifts. Now
your gaze goes elsewhere.
You are not
touching, not cruel.

Arc

My seatmate on the late-night flight
could have been my father. I held
a biography, but he wanted to talk.
The pages closed around my finger
on my spot, and as we inclined
into the sky, we went backwards
in his life, beginning with five hours
before, the funeral for his only brother,
a forgotten necktie in his haste
to catch this plane the other way
just yesterday, his wife at home
caring for a yellow Lab she'd found
along the road by the olive grove,
and the pretty places we had visited—
Ireland for me, Germany for him—
a village where he served his draft
during the Korean War, and would like
to see again to show his wife
how lucky he had been. He talked
to me and so we held
his only brother's death at bay.
I turned off my reading light,
remembering another veteran
I met in a pine forest years ago
who helped me put my tent up
in the wind. What was I thinking
camping there alone? I was grateful
he kept watch across the way
and served coffee in a blue tin cup.
Like the makeshift shelter of a tent,
a plane is brought down,
but as we folded to the ground,
I had come to appreciate

even my seatmate's breath, large
and defenseless, the breath of a man
who hadn't had a good night's rest.
I listened and kept the poles
from blowing down, and kept
a vigil from the dark to day.

Do You Want to Hold the Baby?

my sister asks, offering him across
    the patio bricks, he who began
        as less than a smear of living blood.

All of me wants to fall upon the brittle reply
    invoked by childless women of a certain age:
        "Oh, no, babies don't like me. Usually,

I make them cry." "Here," I will say, thrusting
    the baby back to its mom while lurching
        toward the pinot grigio and diving

into the details of my Greek isles holiday, aquamarine,
    warm nights on the terraces, languid mornings
        stretching into afternoon, silver, coffees, cream.

But I receive her newborn boy. "See," she says. On the edge
    of the swimming pool, my sister and I sit, dipping bare
        legs into the water. One arm under his bottom, the other

on his breathing back, I balance her baby against
    my chest and shoulder. (Is he bigger than a bread
        box?) His dimpled head rolls into the hollow

alongside my jaw. "Remember slumber party
    relay games?" "Remember the one where we passed
        an orange down a line of girls, using only our necks

and chins?" My sister is called into the house.
    The guests mill around the buffet table. Alone
        by the pool, I lean my cheek onto her baby's closed eyes.

The baby is not a hot potato. He is an orange
    and a stuffed pillow case. I practiced for this.
        I can't stand up until somebody comes to take him.

Girl with a Playbill

One man's daughter—she was nineteen then,
a mark. Who knew if she had a bad bone?
Did she know a scoundrel from a thug?
She shopped the corner grocery. She made
a few close friends. After *Les Misérables*
outside the marquee, the rain had nearly stopped.
She skirted oily puddles, thinking the thing
she'd thought since she could remember—
she wished to sing, not how anyone can sing,
but well enough to sing on stage. She knew
that once she drove along the avenues
she'd sing. He reached her as she buckled in.
She didn't push the lock although the thought
occurred. He had a tale. Don't they all.

Monkey with a Cup

Impostor cocktail girl, I could work
my cherry spikes, my little showboat skirt,
the call order—water, seven, soda, coke—
as good as any lifer. I played the flirt
artfully. My name was "Honey" and so was theirs,
those high rollers, handle pullers, and spinners
of wheels. Among the time-defying mirrors,
the din of lights and dollar coins, dirtier
with each exchange, I circulated and sang
my "Cocktails!" mimicry, peddling booze
for silver peanuts. I knew better. A game
like that has just one end: you lose.
But I liked it, just like I like hard candy.
See me, feed me, thank me. Believe me.

Looking for Z—

The lead singer takes the stage, proclaims,
"You won't go home alone."
He's not talking to *us*. We're the married
couple, negotiating our margaritas,
jostled by the young.
We haven't heard from your son Z—
in several weeks. This place
could be his haunt. "Z—
would like this band," you say,
as the mad bass player jumps over
a pot-leaf pumpkin candle-lantern.
You think you spot his friend,
that spiky hair and monster jaw.
"Hey," I shout, but he merely stares.
I wish he were Z—'s friend, for you.
(Where else might a punk-rock god
be tonight? Busing it to San Francisco,
connected to tubes in the ER,
at the other bar next door?)
In the ladies' room, I meet eyes
with a tall, slim girl flourishing
a mascara wand. Have you seen Z—?
I want to ask. She drifts into the past.
The four words of our question
play in my head, a refrain,
as we push our way out the door,
as we beacon home, after you fall into bed,
as I run the bathwater, remembering—
as I do, as I will—age twenty-one—
the fleshy dance-club hours, a man's
glutinous voice, his car, his futon,
my knowledge, my choice,
my choice, my choice. *Have you seen Z—?*

my own parents haven't known to ask.
And as the steam ascends the glass,
my finger's smudge reveals
an eye, a lid, a lash.

Night Rescue

The dog interrupted our argument, the kind
that fishtails, as a car on black ice
skids closer to a precipice—
Will it ever stop? Yes, the mind
suggests, *with the other's death.* That kind.
But the dog offered herself as sacrifice,
tottering thumps along the hall, twice
falling before we could reach her to find
the matter. Her splayed legs wouldn't bend.
She shook, rigid, throat straining to plea,
but no sound would come. "What do
we do for her?" I asked you. "Put an end
to her misery," I thought your answer would be.
Instead, you brought her blanket, and you
laid her on her side. You
tucked in her errant tail, and rubbed her chest
until she softened. Then we got undressed.
In bed, ribs to ribs, pressed,
we heard our dog commence her licks and checks.
Your chin nudged my nose lodged against your neck.

First Thing This Morning

For once I'd like to walk across this floor
without sticking to it, I think on my way
to the coffee pot. Squatting with damp paper
towel, I swipe at gin stains, strawberry
asterisks, my glasses-missing near sight
fixing next on a greasy Rorschach blot
a square away, where from my kneeling height
I can see clear into that awful half-inch slot
between the stove and the cupboard, a treasury
of muck. I sit. All these years
together, we haven't been cleaning. Merely
rearranging. I can't explain these tears.
What is sad about fallen strands of hair,
plastic twistees, and sun-swirling dust in the air?

Come Dusk

I love us when you are not seeking love
on a warm day at the ocean, getting naked,
and plunging in the surf. And I am naked
on our blanket on the sand, doing what I love,

reading a book about places, and things, and love.
I love you when I remember I am naked,
coming up from the page to spot your body, naked,
weightless in the waves, doing what you love.

We will never run hand in hand in white
across the gloss of a travel brochure, and when
the dolphins come at dusk, we will not swim
with them. Against yours, you weigh their might,

and I prefer their distant sight. I love us when
we choose the same by different means. Our days dim.

The Art Teacher's Wife

"Ourselves we do inter with sweet derision."
—*Emily Dickinson*

In the yard, her dog barked along the dark fence.
Next door, the skinny sisters' father swore a blue storm.
The skinny sisters breathed their shallow breaths.
The dog worried a path over sagebrush. Nobody shushed
the dog. How was it I knew the art teacher's wife?
I'd dress and move within those rooms.
She'd worked on painting a vase, the dog at her feet.
To her friend on the phone, the art teacher said,
"She's around here somewhere. I'll see if I can
dredge her up." She took the receiver, making
her voice bright. He rumpled her hair.
Was it that way? They didn't arrive at the faculty party.
I knew her the way the fence's outer side
knows its inner side. Only that it has an inner side.
When the skinny sisters knocked, she invited them in.
Her dog licked their hands. He found them
some rocks to paint. She loved him in that hour,
while the skinny sisters laughed as if
they were children. But their mother made them
return the rocks. She stood in the closet, choosing
something. It was that way, anticipating morning
when she'd drink coffee and read, the warm dog there.
The teacher would sleep. They were on their way
to the party. Her arms held herself across her stomach,
fingers forking into her wrists. Was it always that way?
They braked behind a car ascending the hill. Please
not this time, she spoke into her empty room.
She clutched her shallow breath as they crossed
the double-yellow lines. That wasn't the accident.
Along the fence, her dog went quiet.

"What was that?" the younger sister asked
across the dark. "Dad," her sister said. They listened
to him empty pellets on the countertop. "Only the air gun,"
the older sister whispered. I don't know what happened
to the skinny sisters. They must be teenage girls now.
That wasn't the accident. She read directions.
I knew her in the way we know the things so lived with,
we do not see them—our kneecaps,
the batting around our hearts.
They came out of the canyon. She touched
his forearm. Turn right at the stop sign, she said.
You don't have to tell me, he said, and as he veered,
she opened the door and stepped out.
I heard the way we hear—in splinters.
They said she cracked her head on the pavement.
How awful for the art teacher, they always said.
Blood was on no one's hands and no one saw it
coming. Could it have been that way? I ask
her dog while I rub my hands into sweet fur.
The dog stays quiet and licks my wrists. Good wrists.

Calla Lily

Alone on the bus that night, she was not thinking,
One day I will be a girl I used to know,
was not thinking, *I miss San Francisco,*
was not trying to remember riding
home from the Marina Grill as on any working
night. The bus climbed through the Presidio.
She sat midway back by a dark window,
watching the empty barracks' lights sliding
over glass. She had not left anyone stranded
on a dock. She was no one's morning dream.
And when the driver braked beside the trees,
and went wading through heart-shaped leaves,
returning with a calla lily, she was just a girl he picked
a flower for. She hadn't known it was memory.

II.

Faces at a Play

Teens bluster into the school theater
after fast-food lunches, high-fiving over
seatbacks, snapping gum, not yet aware
of sacred space. Like people everywhere,
they care about whom they get to sit next to
and that there is nothing they have to do.
Dark descends. Now all thoughts are safe
from the betrayal of one's face,
so they bend toward the light. A photograph
shows the incandescence of a laugh,
the splash, when they all dive into the same
deep pool, leaving behind dummy faces
to mark the places where they will surface
when the house lights burble up.

Dumb

But the babysitter said, "Lick
the porch railing." We watched her flick
an ash onto the snow, air thick

with her mouth's steam. Sugary frost
laced the black rail. My brother crossed
his arms. "Girls first," he said. I lost

right from wrong. I put my tongue
on the ice-hot iron. Tears stung
my eyelids. Unseeing, I hung

by my dumb cut tongue. I despised
my feet in their fool, over-sized
boots. My brother, galvanized,

fetching a glass, poured a waterfall
over the rail, releasing me. A pall
came between us. I was a small

stain. Nobody likes to be near
the betrayed. The sitter kept clear.
"You should've known better," my dear

brother said. It was *I* who consoled
him. Absolving him of the cold
backbite of his treachery, I told

him I *did* know better. Good girl,
dumb, chilled, little sister, when will
you make iron of your own will?

Name Pinned to the Skin of a Mole

      I burrow
to the surface of the dream
of barely making it—
such as arriving unprepared
for work, late to the getaway car,
or left without a stretch partner
after everyone has paired,
big underwear creeping
inside my leotard. I'm not well
put together, and everyone can tell.

      Shame to utter
a dirty word, to think
a mean thought, to bleed
onto the plastic school seat.
Shame when a zipper breaks.
Shame to make a mistake.

      My grandmother says, "Don't
be hysterical," when she really means,
"Don't feel." Ancient queen
with her perfect pear.

      Shame is imposed
by those who are supposed to love us
—such as ourselves.

      My mole,
meet your mole: shake,
sniffle, sniffle. Hello.

Catch

When Jim built model rocket ships, his tongue
massaged his inner cheek as if to turn
a crank. We thought this trait was his among
our kin until we watched his daughter learn

to paint, one little cheek out-popped, as sheep
with wings took flight. Jim's depressed again.
If not for Cass, says Emily, he'd sleep
through day and orbit night with science fiction,

untethered by lawless serotonin.
I, too, was misdirected there, where
every star gets smudged. We'll pilot him.
Em names the drug that tempered her despair.

A sort of torch brazing lets gravity
take hold. A battened hatch yields liberty.

Anniversary

A mongrel dog was cast to space to test
for human flight. We've managed fifty years.
Khrushchev, riding on the flaunted crest
of Sputnik's conquest, ordered engineers
to launch a new great thing to celebrate
the Revolution of '17. They called
her Laika. Photogenic—these acts mandate—
she's boarded, one ear cocked, open-jawed.
The public loves a dog who smiles—how brave.
Fur-gloved forepaws cross in the earth-flung jar,
her space. There are no heroes. Only slaves.
It was so loud inside the oven, so far
from home, where our makers forge the story
of betrayal. We name it glory.

Stray Home

i.
I wonder what kind of older woman I'll be.
Will I make weekly trips for wash and set,
pinky brown dye, the ritual of coffee
and chemicals, mirrors and magazines?
Or will I let my hair be what it will
(stuff of granite and wool, tough on a brush),
defiant, not proud, fearing the beautician's
chair and the small talk required there?
Will I think the young girls have time yet
to go around their block, expect them
to drop in on me with tickets to the symphony?
Or will I hover behind their storylines,
pocketing the plots that might have been mine?
And when I am old, what then will I wonder?

ii.
When I was ten, I admired my mother's legs,
so smooth where I touched the curve of the calf.
I'm surprised she let me. She might have
pushed my hand away, making an "ugh"
puff of reproach, as she did when I displayed
my latest trick, a pretty red ring I made
on my wrist, simply by sucking. I was not
to behave that way. She didn't say why not.
I wasn't learning very well because
there was also that time when I lay face down
on my bed, scissoring my thighs like angel wings,
calling, "Mom! Try this. It feels so good."
She singed me to the core: "Don't do that
anymore." I didn't. For a good long time.

iii.
You once confided, "I can remember
as young as six, walking the long way home
from school to avoid meeting my mother."
What could she have taken from you then?
You said, "When she scolded, *Pull up your socks*,
they became her socks, no longer mine."
A girl dreamed of escape with each step
of a scuffed saddle shoe.

                    I can remember
sixteen years old, the one time I skipped
school, I chose to go home. Oh Mom,
I *wanted* to meet you. Opening the door,
I fell into a symphony's deep sea,
flooding the front hall and up the stairs.
Awash, in your bed, I found you dreaming.

iv.
Mt. Fuji, Japan

I hadn't seen my grandma nude, nor she
me, but we didn't comment. A bath
was easier than a tea ceremony,

easier than sashimi, or a path
of finely raked sand. We found
our private moments in the public bath,

arranged as stones in a garden, day drowned.
The other women nodded and closed their eyes.
I saw my grandma's tummy, a small round

pouch, like mine. My mother's breasts were the size
of her own cupped hands, or of one another.
I can't imagine having otherwise.

We were three candle boats—my grandmother,
mother, and me—moored, we bobbed together.

v.
A bird begins a racket out my window—
one of us will have to move—it's me.
So starts her letter, never mind hello;
instead, she whips up a drama, adds whimsy,
even if she must invent the bird,
the window, the racket—because what she means
is *I'm alive and curious.* She's lured
you here; now she must perform. She preens
her words, rehearsing them before they'll show
as she does her clothes before a mirror.
How's this? *On Saturdays, we go*
to funerals and then we go to dinner.
Oh, dear. Her hand tires. She wants to be done.
Bowing out, she writes, *The bird won.*

vi.
Then she sells her ivy-locked home
and comes to California to live among
her daughter's family, those six in the frame
that left a dark square where it had hung
over the stair, where she had glanced going
up and down, and loved them from a distance,
knowing them hardly at all. Unpacking
her white linens, she finds the frame. What sense
in hanging the picture now? The girls arrive,
animating tanned flesh and sun-wide faces,
arrange poppies in a glass, are gone by five,
busy ladies, laughing in between embraces.
Her daughter, in the kitchen quite forgotten,
cleans the icebox, one eye for something rotten.

vii.
Awake, once more, she draws a breath, and draws
a breath. Fog nudges her window screen,
offers dizzy scents of eucalyptus
and salt, says, *Hello, you old string-bean.*
Ah, what to do about today? Really,
it should be some other's turn at this mess.
They say she's not ready to go. Fiddle-dee.
This bed could use a warm back to press
her cold toes against. Her toes know
what time it is. Yet. She likes good wool
and well-made clothes, lunch under a willow,
glass of sherry, rye crisp, Swiss cheese full
of holes. Enough. The coffee pot won't
percolate itself. You show up, or you don't.

viii.
At last the daughter stays the nights
beneath the clock. Tock, tock,
tock, tock. She listens, listens,
from her couch cradle. Does she hear
her mother's breathing heave and drop?
Rising, she crosses a swath of light.
At the bed she kneels, taking in
old, old hair and skin,
moth-thin, rosebud pajamas
and bobby pins. She bends to tuck
the blanket up. Her mother's heart
murmurs and sways, a treetop of leaves.
She is her daughter's broken cup,
her metronome, and frail end stop.

Carsick on the Way to the Coast, with Mary and Her Daughter in the Infant Seat

The hills unfold and green meets blue.
Your baby observes the cows recede.
My sister, new mom, I miss you
(those hills so green I sink in blue),
your ten-speed bike, your running shoes,
and all ways else we used to compete.
The hills parade to spite my blue.
Your baby watches roads recede.

Seesaw

Unnerved by spitting seeds into our picnic grass,
I abandon my slice of watermelon.

My father eats the pulp and seeds down to the white rind.
Mahalo, he offered when I lost my job—

his spin on the Hawaiian thank you—no worries, it's all good.
Nirvana is for those who think like that. I worry.

Not about getting to an afterlife, but that I haven't yet got *here*.
What do you do with a canoe without a paddle?

A mosquito drills for blood before I swat it off my shin.
We're quiet as the lake turns to glass, stained pink at dusk.

My father is going to Argentina next week. Mahalo.
He slices his thumb with his pocketknife. I drive his truck after all,

this time the fittest, my father buckled in beside me,
squeezing a bandanna around his elevated thumb.

He'll tweeze out the stitches in Tucumán, and I'll have moved on.
When he returns, he'll assume I'll call with my coordinates.

Safebox

She drove. It snowed. She drove
inside a snowship, flakes
tunneling toward the windshield
like stars in space movies. No taillights
in front, no headlights behind.
No passenger. Where
were the naked girls, oiled, lit
with neon, now? And all the rum?
What about the parking lot?
The black distance to the rear entrance,
worn carpet, and ripped chairs?
Smother it with the truck-cab heater.
Now this simple capsule. Like the one
in the play-yard with wheels painted on.
There passed an unplowed exit. Christ
and splintered ice.
But her fleece-lined coat on the bench seat.
She broke her mother's nose, running
toward her. The wonder. Blame
deflected. Allowed a child's next day.
She blinked. She said aloud, It will be
okay. She drove. It snowed.

III.

How to Be the Lady of the House

They live together in a house
of their own, and all they have they share
with you: the key the father closes
your hand around, a place at their table
the daughter sets, their pillows
and their books. You will pay attention
to how they do things here. Listen.
"We have three names we call the dog.
We leave our boots in the hall.
When we sing, we harmonize.
Do you prefer John or Paul?
All you have to do is love us back.
On school mornings, you can help
with honey tea and ponytail,
and send us out the door." Now
you will turn in your sock feet.
The dog eyes you from his rug.
You are very quiet. You open the closet.
Coats with pockets of candy bits
and crumpled leaves from seasons past
wait for arms to fill them.
Come on. You can hang your slicker
beside the pink-and-yellow jacket
and the overcoat you will recognize
as the one the father wore the day
you met him. There. You are practicing.
Take your cue from the child, who leaves
her bed at dawn to play the piano.
Allowing you and her father
all the wealth of each other's warmth,
she is unafraid to fill a sleeping house
with the blundering joy of just-learned song.

The Donut Shop

I stood before the bakery's donut case,
eyeing the plump mounds, yellow-lit,
ordered on their trays, oozing sweetness,

jelly-filled, glazed, and sprinkled, each a ticket.
The rounded glass was thick and smooth,
and when the clerk did not appear, it didn't

matter because I couldn't speak or choose.
Those days were like that.
The dizzy, rose-warm smell loose

beneath the glass. I toiled to penetrate,
so close, as when under the quilted cover,
my arm across his chest, I pressed against

my love's back, all that's good as near
as that. I took nothing. Turning my face
from the pane, I broke past the elbowed chatter

of the donut eaters, the clink of spoons, lace
of sugar on upper lips, the door-chime's false
farewell. A dog waited in front of the place.

She sniffed my proffered wrist, found my traitor pulse.

Postcards from the Best Women Friends of Our Men

Infiltrating through the mail slot
every few months,
the postcards arrive,
four corners of pride,
pictures of some place exotic—
Paris streetside, cable car—
or of something erotic—
pen-and-ink female nude's
round ass saying,
I do know you so,
thick, flared handwriting
saying, I am never far,
my love to Beth, Anna,
or Liz saying, I have nothing
to hide.
        We set them
on the entry table to be
casually commented on.
For weeks they turn up
around our households,
riding a stack of bills,
collecting egg stains
on the counter, waiting
to be accounted for.
        Although the postcards
may as well be acrylic handprints
on our walls, we muster
our more excellent selves.
Funny Val or Marla, we say.
My, my. And just as they do,
we wonder what it's like to be
the one who might have been.

After Being Elsewhere,
Upon Returning

Home. A line of dust on the table lamp,
teaspoons waiting in the rack, a stack of books
I meant to read, car keys hanging on the hook,
a leaf fallen off the umbrella plant,
and through the blind, afternoon's narrow slant,
shifted a few degrees in the window nook,
where I sit, my suitcase packed with things I took,
sweaters, tousled, and socks, balled and damp

as evidence. What of this bird flying
figure eights in my throat? What of the world whistling,
yet, still there? How do I make room
for the streets and meals and ticket stubs, swinging
doors, and different skin? Why won't this winging
alight? Look here, migrant girl. You're home.

The Grizzly Bear in February

Soulard, St. Louis

A man and a woman came into the restaurant
just after three, the dead hour. He had coffee,
black, and she wanted soup and oyster crackers
and hot tea. They stayed after I brought the tab,
so I went to their booth with the coffee pot
in one hand and the teapot in the other,
but the man said, "No more for me,"
and the woman said, "I'd float out of here,"
putting her hand over the top of her cup.
They would let me know when they wanted to pay.
I sat at the bar rolling napkins. Orvin
tuned the kitchen radio to an R & B station.
I listened to him sing as he prepped food,
and I listened to the man and the woman in the booth.
Then the woman was saying, "He hurled the plate
of food against the wall. It just missed my head."
I turned on my stool. Her companion
bit his lip and shook his head from side to side.
I realized they had been speaking of a person
they both knew well, someone they loved,
someone who loved them—I was sure of it.
And this loved person was laid up in bed,
and had been for some months. "He shouted,
'You dumb selfish bitch. You stupid female.'"
The woman did not alter the flat tone of her voice.
I rolled another napkin. "I went in the basement
and closed the door. I could still hear him.
I read the dials on the washer—gentle spin
and regular cycle." She gave a small laugh.
"On the shelf there was that bird feeder he'd made.
You know the one in the shape of a cottage
with the chimney and the round door?"

"I've got one, too," the man said.
"I have my dignity," the woman went on.
"I wanted to go back in, to go to him,
but I wouldn't." There was a pause. The man
took his wallet from his back pocket. "He's afraid,
you know," the man said. "It's because he's scared."
"I know. I know," the woman said. "I'll get the tip."
I watched the man hold the door for the woman.
Orvin sat beside me and smoked. I finished
the napkins and stacked them in the basket.
"You might as well go on home, pretty lady,"
Orvin said. I told him to call me if he needed
me to come back. I knew he wouldn't need me.
The day was already darkening. I got my coat
from behind the bar. The front door shoved open.
The woman from the booth hurried toward us.
"I may have left something," she said.
"Did you find an envelope, with some legal papers,
a will, to be exact?" I hadn't found anything,
but I went to the booth with her. She checked
the floor under the table and she ran her fingers
between the booth-back and the bench.
People were always leaving their things in the bar.
We kept a drawer of credit cards and lone earrings.
Orvin wrote her name and number on a cocktail napkin.
There was nothing left to do. I already had my coat on.
I walked out with the woman. It was dark now.
It was time to go home. "He was right," the woman said.
"Stupid me. Losing his will." She made another
of her small laughs. I was supposed
to say something comforting. I could have said
that anyone can misplace something. But I didn't think
things would turn up for her before they got worse.
Inside the bar, I saw Orvin watching the television.
The woman tightened her scarf. We were stuck
at the window. Along the street, brick chimneys
sent up smoke and hearths gathered ash.

The Lafayette Square
Holiday Mansion Tour

I lost a glove on the mansion tour.
Perhaps I let it fall.
I had a pair, and then, one fewer.

Grasping a walnut banister,
we gazed three stories tall.
I lost my glove on the mansion tour,

or did I leave it there? A door
withdrew within a wall.
What was a pair was then one fewer.

Golden blooms on velvet paper
yellowed along the hall.
I dropped my glove on that mansion tour.

If it's found and cached in a parlor drawer,
who dares to pay a call
to claim the match that is one fewer?

In paper bags, white candles flicker
around the grand old mall.
I lost a glove on the mansion tour.
Hand in hand, we left, one fewer.

Duet Under Glass

Long after the prior moment,
I soak in a salmon-pink bath

while ice-block glass, this room's
luxury, polarizes the summer.

Warm, salted, I am my witness:
floating torso, futile limbs.

Who lives in here?
Whose foot of five

coral nails? There is the vase carried
from the other sill. Grim neck.

Where is the moment when other
outcomes were still possible?

I took those old stairs two at a time,
the dog arched into greeting,

our spine-bent books—naïve props—
held steady. Catch her,

I urge. Now. Now.
A single hair grips the porcelain.

Daughter for My Prayer

After Weldon Kees

I spot my daughter on the stage and blush
with love. She is my own scrub weed among
other curious shoots. I watch her rush
to board a train and grasp a made-up rung.
Her dad's white shirttails hang below her knees.
One hand to ear, she's answering a cell.
Now rubbing her temples, she acts displeased.
(Why am I cold?) She plays the part so well.
Oh may she never board that lonely car,
nor tread the frozen ground of foul mistakes.
At last, searching the shadowed crowd, she takes
her bow—my honey, restored. There we are:
her dad and his ex. Unwind this song I've sung.
I have no daughter. She could be anyone.

Pink Cotton Panties
& the Bonsai Tree

When I watched
him watch
the pig-tailed
child
turn upside down
over the café railing,
her rose-flecked panties
playing peek-a-boo,
he looked & looked away
toward the cloud castles,
a private smile
glinting on his lips,
& later he asked
how I was doing
with my little essay,
attaching "bunny"
to my name,
that's when
I bit
the *bunjinki* wire.

Shudder

Behind the bathroom's high-up windowpane,
a ragged V of winter geese skimmed past
the naked maple's silver branch, so fast
that had I not stepped in—just then—to hang
the laundered things and pull the curtain's chain,
I would have seen the branches only, glassed
and undesigned, and missed the flight's contrast,
the fallen bird that fluttered to regain
a place. The summer she sent Nan and Scott
to music camp, naked on a lawn chair,
Mrs. O'Donnell slept. Our live oak leaned
into their yard. I watched from our back stair.
Then Nan was killed before she turned eighteen.
How marred our distant naps, how not uncaught.

Embrace on the Neck

After The Prodigal Son and His Father
by George Grey Barnard
Sculpture in marble, 1904

But when he was a great way off, his father saw him, and had
compassion and ran, and fell on his neck, and kissed him.
—*Luke 15:20*

I did not return home.
My father fetched me home.
I was lifted from my knees
by the strength of my father.

Under the breadth of the father,
the son is brought to his knees.
He will not collapse.
His haunches support
the weight of the father.

I have come home.
Under the lamp of my father,
I am fed steak and milk.
My shoulders tighten into knots.

Under the arm of the father,
the son's head is pressed.
He is sunk to his senses
under the weight of the father.
The son's spine strains
into the soft pulp of the buttocks
under the bulk of the father.

I lie down to sleep
under the roof of my father,

knees brought close to my chest.
I lie down to sleep
before the new day's questions
from my father.

What will you do?
How much do you need?
When will you go?

The Roasted-Corn Man of Golden Hill

A reason? Nobody is asking here,
alongside Mexico, trailing sand across
thresholds, under thin leaves of the pepper
trees. On Thursday nights, the neighbor boys

heft baskets of the family laundry
from the rusted Ford's trunk while their mama
gives orders in her last clean skirt. Their sister,
gazing from the bench—a hemangioma,

a perfect red plum, disfiguring a cheek—
tips her popsicle toward my shy dog, caught
between scent and the shelter of my legs.
The quarter-a-window washer works the lot,

climbing onto hoods with his spray bottle,
headlines, and classified ads. Nobody
is expecting anything nor waiting
to be disappointed. The fig tree

provides ample shade beneath wide
branches. They're painting the market
banana yellow with fat green stripes,
like the saltwater taffy sold at the trinket

shops by the docks where the Navy boats
maneuver home and pedi-cabbies beckon.
The mechanic says he'll fix my timing,
in a cadence that could as well say, "Listen.

There's a place on the couch beside me.
I would love our child more than life. Here's
a spoon for your chocolate. Come now, don't cry."
There is nothing the nectar of gentleness

fails to soothe. The ex-convict crawls
from his sleeping bag in his dad's yard.
He says good morning to the flip-flop girls
leaving their apartment in their postcard

skirts, like butterflies. He's carried
their TV up the stairs. The clouds disperse,
and at the bottom of the salty hill,
the waves, shiny-buckle-topped, rehearse—

you're it, come get me, you're it, come get me.
I smell the corn roasting on the vendor's grill
as I gather my bakery-warm clothes
from the dryer. It's not impossible,

after all, to arrive, intact—yet far
from where one thought to be—slip in
and resume, while the roasted-corn man
spits tobacco through his chapped half-grin.

Neighbors

I got up in the night.
My dog came along.
The rooms made arms.
I poured a glass of water.
My dog drank from her bowl.
Through the window screen,
I heard my neighbor breathing
and wind chimes jingling
from a nail in his foyer.
"That's Dave," I said to my dog.
His bedroom adjoined mine.
The holidays were coming
and neither of us had a boyfriend.
I gave my dog a biscuit.
She was scheduled to die
in the morning at nine o'clock.
I looked in the cupboards
for something more.
I saw the reliable plates.
Earlier, Dave and I drank
the wine he was saving for a date.
"Ah hell," he said, and I agreed.
My dog went to the door.
I let her out to the courtyard.
I stood in the front room, waiting.
The white lamp hovered in the corner
like a moonfish. Out there, my dog
would wince when she squatted
but her nose would work
the soft air. I knew that.
I got up in the night.
Rooms were like arms,
lamps like fish, and morning
approached like the milk truck,
though we don't see those anymore.

Apology to the Foster Child
on Her Tenth Birthday

You wanted a doll baby
that coos and cries, one
who takes a bottle, one
who needs a battery.
Through plastic-windowed boxes,
the babies watched. Not one

that cooed and cried could be
your baby. The brown one
only blinked. One
collective voice rebuked me:
Who gives a blue-eyed
child to a brown-eyed one?

I left without a baby.
You were too old for one
anyway. Someone
your age wants snappy
sparkle rollershoes.
I wrapped the bright pink ones.

While blinking tears away,
you laced a shoe. Stray one,
I enfolded you. Everyone
needs to feel necessary.
The dolls endured the shelf.
You reached for your favorite one.

Shell Pink Clock

Perfectly round. Thin gold
hands chart its public face.
Cut-glass lamp, teardrop chain.
And a flat, black skipping stone.

Objects of her bedside, arranged
from before. Stone of hope,
lamp of mercy, clock of love.
One year more. Hard bare floor.

Our Friends in Minnesota

A woman (I would be her) says
to a man (he would be you),
"Let's go stay with Ted and Jan."

And what are Ted and Jan?
Ted and Jan are our friends
who live by the lake in Duluth.

They have beautiful teenage daughters.
Tanya, the older one, plays the cello.
Shelly captains the Irish dance team.

Ted and Jan have invited us up
to sail with them anytime we want.
Late June is good. In the evening,

we play cards on their screened deck.
Crickets. Cocktails. Tanya comes down
and drapes over the back of Ted's chair,

her arms around his shoulders. "Daddy,
I see you're losing again," she teases.
"Where's the love?" Ted says, and Jan

flourishes another full house. Her cheeks
are reddened from the day on the boat.
Later, we listen to Ted strum the guitar,

and we talk of food and people we know.
When Shelly isn't in by eleven, we hear
of the boy she's taken up with,

the one who threw up in the lilac bushes
outside their window. "He's a good kid,
though," Ted says. Jan arches one eyebrow,

as she's always done. But here's
Shelly now, chiming, "I'm home."
Is it too much to say I'm happy,

viewing from my deck chair, my arms
around my knees? Tucked in the attic bed,
you and I hold hands and giggle and talk

about Ted and Jan. I made them up,
and I made up you. The old boards
shift and settle, as dreamers do.

Winter and the Santa Ana Winds

Late December, and the dry Santa Ana winds
      return, sever bark from the palms,

shatter the bulbs of the crèche balancing
      on the roof of Brian's American Eatery,

split my thumb skin. Apprenticed
      to unflappability, I

negotiate the crosswalk, cover my coffee lid,
      spit hair from my mouth,

scan peripheries, devise my plan
      for not if/then, but when/

then. I prefer my tears this way,
      whipped sideways and seared off.

Brush ignites.
      The Santas Anas lick the flames.

I hasten home. Needles from the Christmas tree
      scatter to the floor.

Far away north and east of here, snowfall quiets a road.
      There's a room with a bed, a lamp,

and a wood outside a windowpane. My new love,
      are you there? I will come to you.

I will come only to you shedding vigilance. Snow lies down
      on the branches. Branches hold.

Why We Love Our Dogs

Once, while walking, I happened
across a woman throwing rocks
into a creek pool for a dog to fetch.
Each time, the dog—a muscled, golden
pit bull—plunged into the green
water and searched, in vain,
for the rock, which had, meanwhile, sunk.
The woman coaxed her dog to the shore.
Then, she tossed another rock. Again, straight
into the creek followed the very good dog.
Earlier, over sandwiches, a friend I hadn't seen
in quite some time, told me of another friend
I hadn't seen in a long time. Our friend,
three times married, now single, and in love,
was moving to another state to join a man
in his hometown. There was nothing
we could say without appearing to judge,
we agreed. Anyway, she'd still go!
Once, somebody told me dogs lack a sense of time.
Five minutes, five years—it's all the same to them.
I find this hard to believe. Still, that night,
while driving home in a steady downpour,
I made up a dog. We quivered
with bedrock faith. I'd be there, in no time at all.

NOTES

"Stray Home" is in memory of Alice Kovar Goldstein.

Bunjinki wire in "Pink Cotton Panties & the Bonsai Tree" refers to the copper or aluminum wire used to train a *bunjin-* or *literati-*style bonsai tree.

"Embrace on the Neck" is inspired by *The Prodigal Son and His Father* by George Grey Barnard, sculpture in marble, 1904, the Speed Art Museum, Louisville, Kentucky.

"Neighbors" borrows its first line from Elizabeth Bishop's poem "The Riverman."

The opening clause of "Why We Love Our Dogs" echoes lines in Scott Cairns' poem "The Theology of Delight" in his collection *Philokalia*.

LaVergne, TN USA
15 March 2010
175928LV00002BA/1/P